SUPER FUNNY SCHOOL JOKES

by Gene Perret

ILLUSTRATED by
Sanford Hoffman

 Sterling Publishing Co., Inc.   New York

Library of Congress Cataloging-in-Publication Data

Perret, Gene.
    Super funny school jokes / Gene Perret ; illustrated by Sanford
Hoffman.
        p.   cm.
    Includes index.
    Summary: An illustrated collection of jokes about school, from the
first day to the last test.
    ISBN 0-8069-8294-2 (trade)
    1. Education—Juvenile humor.   2. Wit and humor, Juvenile.
[1. Jokes.   2. Schools—Wit and humor.]   I. Hoffman, Sanford, ill.
II. Title.
PN6231.S3P46   1991
818'.5402—dc20   91-22501
                                                                CIP
                                                                 AC

10   9   8   7   6   5   4   3

First paperback edition published in 1992 by
Sterling Publishing Company, Inc.
387 Park Avenue South, New York, N.Y. 10016
© 1991 by Gene Perret
Distributed in Canada by Sterling Publishing
% Canadian Manda Group, P.O. Box 920, Station U
Toronto, Ontario, Canada M8Z 5P9
Distributed in Great Britain and Europe by Cassell PLC
Villiers House, 41/47 Strand, London WC2N 5JE, England
Distributed in Australia by Capricorn Link Ltd.
P.O. Box 665, Lane Cove, NSW 2066
Manufactured in the United States of America
All rights reserved

Sterling ISBN 0-8069-8294-2 Trade
             0-8069-8295-0 Paper

CONTENTS

To
Marianne,
Tommy,
Kevin,
and
Gerard

Why do some fish swim on the bottom of the sea?
That's where fish go when they drop out of school.

1.
THE FIRST DAY OF SCHOOL

The first day of school is always special to me. It's the only day of the year when I'm not behind in my homework.

★ ★ ★

The first day of school wouldn't be so bad if it weren't followed by the second day of school, and the third day of school, and then the fourth day of school . . .

★ ★ ★

The first day of school is exciting, but so is riding a roller coaster—and I wouldn't want to do that for nine months in a row, either.

★ ★ ★

Teachers always seem happy on the first day of school. That's because they're getting paid to be there. We kids have to do it for free.

★　★　★

Show me a kid who likes the first day at school and I'll show you a kid who likes to get his lip caught under a manhole cover.

★　★　★

There's one good thing about the first day of school—when it's over, you're one day closer to the last day of school.

★　★　★

Some kids enjoy buying school supplies. To me, it's like buying your own dental instruments.

★　★　★

One of my classmates gets carried away. He shows up for the first day of school each year with a smiling face and three pack mules of school supplies.

I show up at the beginning of each school year with a full pencil box and an empty head.

★   ★   ★

I love school supplies. If only there were some other place we could use them besides school.

★   ★   ★

My grandparents buy me so many school supplies for the first day of school that I have to take the first two weeks off just to sharpen pencils.

★   ★   ★

I buy pencils with an eraser at both ends. That's so I can make sure I don't make the same mistake twice.

★   ★   ★

JOHNNY: Teacher, I don't have a pencil.
TEACHER: How can you come to school without a pencil?
JOHNNY: I took the bus.

★   ★   ★

JOHNNY: Teacher, I don't have a pencil.
TEACHER: I want you to write 100 times, "I will come to school prepared."
JOHNNY: With what?

★   ★   ★

MOTHER: Now those are the kinds of clothes I wish I could have worn when I was in school.
DAUGHTER: They were probably in style back then.

★   ★   ★

MOTHER: There now, young man, I think that outfit is absolutely perfect.

JOHNNY: Mom, it's the first day of school; not a Pee Wee Herman look-alike contest.

★　★　★

MOTHER: I want to help you pick out your new school outfits because I want you to buy clothes that last.

JOHNNY: Mom, the clothes you pick out will last forever because I'm never going to wear them.

★　★　★

MOTHER: Now these new clothes are expensive. I don't want you coming home from school that first week with a hole in the knee.

JOHNNY: Okay, Mom, where would you like the hole?

★　★　★

I don't know how my Mom does it, but she even buys shoelaces that are out of style.

★　★　★

MOTHER: What's wrong with the new clothes I bought you? They're indestructible.

JOHNNY: So is a Sherman tank, Mom, but I wouldn't wear it to school.

★　★　★

Moms like to buy "sensible" clothing. That's the kind that they only sell in the "Junior Nerd" department.

★　★　★

BILLY: What room are you in this year?

JOHNNY: Room 12A.

BILLY: Wait a minute, that's the gymnasium.

JOHNNY: When I registered for school this year, I told them I was a basketball.

★ ★ ★

TEACHER: I'm your teacher this year. My name is Mr. Wilson. Can you all remember that?

JOHNNY: If we can't, we're going to have one heckuva time with the 12-times tables.

★ ★ ★

JOHNNY: I have the toughest teacher in the whole school.

BILLY: How do you know that?

JOHNNY: Last year he flunked himself.

TEACHER: Everybody hand in your homework, please.

JOHNNY: Teacher, it's the first day of school. We didn't have any homework.

TEACHER: That's right, and that's the last excuse for not doing your homework that I'll accept for the rest of the year.

★ ★ ★

BILLY: My teacher this year is Mrs. Wright. They say she rules the fifth grade with an iron fist.

JOHNNY: I believe it. That's the way she plays the piano at school assemblies.

★ ★ ★

TEACHER: I'll be your teacher this year. Does anybody here know my name?

JOHNNY: How do you like that? It's only the first day of school and already we're having a quiz.

★ ★ ★

TEACHER: I'll be teaching you English this year and there are two words that I will not permit on any of your writing assignments. One is "cool" and the other is "lousy."

JOHNNY: Okay, what are the words?

★ ★ ★

JOHNNY: Our teacher is going to be tough this year. We've been instructed to say "Yes, Sir" and "No, Sir."

BILLY: That's not unusual.

JOHNNY: It is when your teacher's a woman.

★ ★ ★

2.
WHAT I DID DURING THE SUMMER

During the summer I just played and had fun all day long—the same as I do during school.

★   ★   ★

This summer, I did absolutely nothing all day. Now I know what it's like to be a teacher.

★   ★   ★

During the summer, my Dad took me to the zoo. They wouldn't accept me, so he had to take me home again.

★   ★   ★

This past summer I learned how to ride a horse and how to eat standing up.

★   ★   ★

TEACHER: And what did you learn during the summer, Herman?

HERMAN: I learned that three months is not enough time to straighten up my room.

★   ★   ★

During the summer my big brother learned how to tie several different things into knots. I was one of the things.

★   ★   ★

Summer camp is a fun place to be—if you're a mosquito.

★   ★   ★

We had big mosquitoes on our vacation. If you swatted them, they swatted you back.

★   ★   ★

I never saw such big mosquitoes. I had one mosquito in my room and he kept me awake all night. He kept pushing me out of bed.

★   ★   ★

This summer I saw the biggest mosquitoes I ever saw in my life. They were so big they came equipped with landing gear.

★   ★   ★

We had huge mosquitoes on our summer vacation. I've seen big mosquitoes before, but these had their own landing strip.

★   ★   ★

I got bitten by so many mosquitoes during my vacation, when I finally got home I had to have a friend come over to help me scratch.

★   ★   ★

The mosquitoes on our vacation were so big that insect repellent didn't bother them. They'd just carry you down to the stream and wash it off.

The mosquitoes on our summer vacation were so big they not only bit you, they also knocked you down and stole your wallet.

★   ★   ★

I wonder—when mosquitoes go on vacation, do they complain about all the people?

★   ★   ★

On our vacation this summer, I saw fireflies for the first time. I didn't know what they were. I thought the mosquitoes were coming after us with flashlights.

★   ★   ★

Parents are funny. They want me to learn how to survive in the wilderness, but they won't let me go to the mall on my own.

★   ★   ★

I slept under the stars for the first time this summer. We didn't go camping; we had our roof repaired.

★   ★   ★

I went to camp this summer and saw a lot of wild animals. In fact, several of them were my cabin mates.

The food was bad at summer camp. I threw my dinner in the river one night and the fish threw it back.

★   ★   ★

Our counselors told my parents that nothing at this camp was poisonous. That was before they tasted the food.

★ ★ ★

The food was so bad at summer camp we used to rub it on our bodies to keep insects away.

★ ★ ★

Some of the kids got sick from the food at camp, but it was their own fault. They ate it.

★ ★ ★

Food fights were encouraged at our summer camp. They were not only fun, but it was safer than eating the food.

★ ★ ★

The chef at our summer camp was dangerous. He had a black belt in cooking.

★ ★ ★

I was sent home from summer camp because of poor eyesight. I was the only camper who didn't see the skunk.

★ ★ ★

During the summer I had a few unpleasant experiences with skunks. They smell a lot like gym class.

★ ★ ★

COUNSELOR: Does anybody here know the difference between a biscuit and a rock?
CAMPER: I do!
COUNSELOR: Good—you're cooking breakfast.

★ ★ ★

CLEM: I know how to tell directions by using the stars.

LEM: So do I. If you're getting closer to them you're going up.

★   ★   ★

During summer camp I never changed my clothes once. Towards the end, the skunks ran away from me.

★   ★   ★

I came home from summer camp with twelve pets that I found in the woods. So far my mother has only found three of them.

★   ★   ★

COUNSELOR: What's the best thing to do to keep from getting lost in the woods?

CAMPER: Stay in your room.

★   ★   ★

COUNSELOR: What side of a tree does moss grow on?

CAMPER: The outside.

★   ★   ★

During the summer I went to a dude ranch. One cowboy there asked me if I ever rode a jackass.

I said, "No."

He said, "Well, you'd better get on to yourself."

★   ★   ★

3.
WHERE DO THEY GO?

Where do hyenas go to school?
Ha-Ha-vard.

★　　★　　★

Where do clocks go to school?
Georgia Tech-tock.

★　　★　　★

Where do convicts go to school?
Penn.

★　　★　　★

What school do snakes go to?
Pitt.

★　　★　　★

What school does Orville Reddenbacher go to?
Pop-Cornell.

★　　★　　★

What school do dogs go to?
BARK-ley.

         ★   ★   ★

What school do cats go to?
PURR-due.

What school did Uncle Ben go to?
Rice.

         ★   ★   ★

What school does Royalty go to?
Duke or PRINCE-ton.

         ★   ★   ★

What school do toothbrushes go to?
Colgate.

         ★   ★   ★

What school do door-to-door salesmen go to?
The school of hard knocks.

★ ★ ★

What school do comedians go to?
The school of hard knock-knock jokes.

★ ★ ★

What school do peeping toms go to?
Peking U.

★ ★ ★

What school do sleepyheads go to?
A NAP-polis.

★ ★ ★

What school is especially for soldiers with a bad sense of direction?
East Point.

★ ★ ★

What school is named after a cattle car?
Ox-Ford.

★ ★ ★

What school do bunny rabbits go to?
Johns HOP-kins.

★ ★ ★

What do they do there?
Play EASTER BASKET-ball.

★ ★ ★

4.
TEACHERS I HAVE KNOWN & ANNOYED

It's not going to school that bothers me so much; it's the principal of the thing.

★   ★   ★

Teachers act like they know all the answers. Why shouldn't they? They're the ones that make up all the questions.

★   ★   ★

TEACHER: I'm surprised. You should know the answer to that question.

SUZIE: Well, maybe I will when I get to be your age.

★   ★   ★

If teachers are so smart, how come their book is the only one with the answers in it?

I have one teacher who is so forgetful he gave the same test three weeks in a row. If he does that two more times, I may pass it.

One of our teachers is a real grouch. He seems to hate school more than we do.

One of our teachers used to be a Drill Instructor in the Marines, but they had to let him go. He was too tough on the guys.

We have one teacher who is so tough, when he calls the roll even kids who are present pretend they're absent.

None of the students likes this one teacher. Last year the kids brought him 37 apples. Only two of them weren't ticking.

I had one teacher who was so absent-minded, once she even forgot to give us grades. It was the highest mark I ever got in that class.

I have one teacher who will accept no excuse for being late to school. I know. I've tried them all.

One of our teachers dislikes kids. On our last exam, we all had points taken off for being under 21.

★ ★ ★

We had one very forgetful teacher. The first thing he did when he came into the classroom was write his name on the blackboard. And every day it was a different name.

★ ★ ★

I have one teacher who doesn't like kids. He says if it weren't for schoolchildren, he could have the rest of the day off.

★ ★ ★

5.
HOMEWORK & OTHER THINGS I DON'T DO

Well, I figured out what I'm going to be doing in my old age—my homework.

★   ★   ★

I have so much homework to do it doesn't leave me any time for my studies.

★   ★   ★

I'm so far behind in my homework that my 2nd grade teacher asked me to bring my parents to school. And I'm in the 5th grade.

★   ★   ★

I'm going to lead a long life. That's the only way I'll ever get caught up on all my homework.

★   ★   ★

TEACHER: That should be enough homework to keep you busy.

WANDA: That should be enough homework to keep the Chinese Army busy.

MICHAEL: Teacher, is there life after death?

TEACHER: Why do you ask?

MICHAEL: I may need the extra time to finish all this homework you gave us.

★   ★   ★

NAN: I have so much homework to finish the teacher said she may send someone to my home.

DAN: To talk to your parents?

NAN: No, to help me carry it to school.

★   ★   ★

I'm so far behind in my homework I may have to drop out of school to finish it.

★   ★   ★

TEACHER: Johnny, what is the definition of "infinity?"

JOHNNY: Tonight's homework assignment.

★   ★   ★

TEACHER: Young man, did you do all your homework last night?

KARL: No, teacher. I did some of it last night, some of it in the middle of the night, and the rest of it early this morning.

★   ★   ★

ROGER: Teacher, this is an awful lot of math homework.

TEACHER: You should be able to complete it if you work hard.

ROGER: Could you throw in one more really hard problem?

TEACHER: Why?

ROGER: It will give my Dad something to do so I can get this done faster.

★   ★   ★

TEACHER: Your homework assignment last night was to draw a map of Texas including all the rivers in that state. Why didn't you finish it?

FRANK: I ran out of paper. I thought you wanted it actual size.

★   ★   ★

TEACHER: Young man, this is the first homework assignment you've handed in all week. Why is that?

RICHARD: I was in a hurry last night and didn't have time to think up a good excuse.

★   ★   ★

One kid in our class always said his dog ate his homework and none of us believed him until last week. His dog graduated from Harvard.

★　★　★

TEACHER: So your dog ate your homework?
ALLAN: Yes, teacher.
TEACHER: And where is your dog right now?
ALLAN: He's at the vet. He doesn't like math any more than I do.

★　★　★

TEACHER: Young woman, where's your homework assignment?
BARBARA: It blew away while I was coming to school.
TEACHER: I see. And why are you late for school?
BARBARA: I had to wait for a heavy wind.

★　★　★

TEACHER: On Monday you said your homework blew away. On Tuesday you said your father accidentally took it to work with him. On Wednesday you said your little sister tore it up. On Thursday you said someone stole it. Today I asked you to bring your parents to school. Now where are they?

WILSON: My dog ate them.

    ★   ★   ★

TEACHER: Young woman, you've told me that your homework blew off your desk and out an open window into the trash. The trash was picked up this morning and you can't retrieve your homework because it is now buried in a nuclear waste dump. Do you really expect me to believe all that garbage?

STEPHANIE: No, but did you really expect me to do all that homework?

    ★   ★   ★

It takes me about two hours each night to do my homework—three if my Dad helps me.

    ★   ★   ★

TEACHER: Anyone who doesn't bring all the homework to class tomorrow morning will get an "F."

TOM: And anyone who does bring all the homework to class tomorrow morning will get a hernia.

    ★   ★   ★

SON: Dad, if an airplane leaves Chicago and flies 500 miles an hour west with a 300 mile-an-hour wind coming East for two hours, and then flies 600 miles an hour with a 100 mile-an-hour wind coming East, and then flies 700 miles an hour for 2 hours with no headwind, how far will that plane have flown?

FATHER: Son, I'll call my office in the morning and have you switch to an easier flight.

TEACHER: Young man, you haven't handed in one homework assignment since we started this class. Won't you please do tonight's assignment?

GEORGE: What? And ruin a perfect record?

★   ★   ★

I have one teacher who is so fanatical, she even gives us extra recess to do at home.

★   ★   ★

6.
TESTS ARE RUINING MY GRADES

Our teacher says that he gives us tests to find out how much we know. Then all the questions are about things we don't know.

★　★　★

Our teacher gives us a test every Friday. The only good thing about it is that it's followed by Saturday and Sunday.

★　★　★

I didn't know anything before I started going to school. I still don't know anything, but now they test me on it.

★　★　★

Our teacher said, "Write your name and today's date on the top of your exam paper. Do it carefully. For many of you it will be the only thing you get right on the entire page."

★ ★ ★

TEACHER: I've given you a multiple-choice exam. What more do you want?
HECTOR: More choices.

★ ★ ★

NAN: I bite my fingernails before easy exams.
DAN: What do you do when you're taking a hard exam?
NAN: Then I bite other people's fingernails.

★ ★ ★

PETRA: Teacher, I get so nervous before an exam that I even forget my own name.
TEACHER: Well, whoever's name you put on this test is flunking the course.

★ ★ ★

Our teacher told us we should do something to help us relax right before taking an exam—so I took a two-week vacation.

★ ★ ★

MUFF: We had a test on the Revolutionary War that was so hard that George Washington would have flunked it.
FLUFF: We had a test last week that was so hard even the teacher flunked it.

★ ★ ★

To me, taking a test is just like going to the dentist, except after the test you don't get a chance to rinse.

★   ★   ★

I used to hate tests. Then my teacher said to just treat them as a game. Now I hate games, too.

★   ★   ★

We had a test yesterday that was so tough, the school nurse had to be present before we could begin.

There's only one thing I hate more than taking tests in school. And that's the grade I get after taking tests in school.

★   ★   ★

MONA: Mom, I don't want to go to school today.

MOM: Why? Have you got a stomachache?

MONA: No.

MOM: Have you got a sore throat?

MONA: No.

MOM: Have you got a headache?

MONA: No.

MOM: What have you got?

MONA: A test in History.

★ ★ ★

My Dad always says "What you don't know won't hurt you." It sure hurt me in the math test I took last week.

★ ★ ★

TEACHER: Name two cities in Kentucky.

STUART: Okay, I'll name one Dave, and the other Irving.

I got a minus-30 on one exam. I not only got the wrong answers, but I misspelled three of them.

★ ★ ★

HARVEY: Teacher, does neatness count on that test we just took?

TEACHER: Yes, it does.

HARVEY: Then I should get a high mark because I didn't write anything on the paper.

★ ★ ★

GLORIA: Teacher, how did I do on yesterday's spelling test?

TEACHER: Let's put it this way—do you know how to spell "F"?

★ ★ ★

I got a 60 on my Map Skills test. That's not bad for a kid who wasn't allowed to cross the street until just a few years ago.

★ ★ ★

DAD: I don't understand your poor History grades. I always did well in History when I was a kid.

DEXTER: Dad, there's a lot more History now than when you were a kid.

★ ★ ★

BILLIE: I'd rather jump off a ten-story building than take this Science test.

WILLIE: I didn't know we had a choice.

★ ★ ★

TEACHER: How many planets are in the sky?

CANDACE: I think all of them.

★ ★ ★

TEACHER: Where do we find the Suez Canal?

HARRY: It should be written right here on my sleeve with the rest of the answers.

* * *

TEACHER: How long did Thomas Edison live?

SYLVIA: All his life.

* * *

TEACHER: When did George Washington die?

REX: It was just a few days before they buried him.

* * *

TEACHER: When did Napoleon die?

TAD: Die? I didn't even know he was sick.

* * *

TEACHER: Can you tell me how long pot roast should be cooked?

LOUELLA: The same as short pot roast.

* * *

TEACHER: You got a perfect zero on your exam. How do you do it?

JACK: It was luck. I guessed at some of the answers.

* * *

TEACHER: What was the pen name of Samuel Clemens?

LOLA: Was it "Bic"?

* * *

TEACHER: What number comes after 4?

VIC: All the rest of them.

* * *

7.

SO MANY SUBJECTS—
SO LITTLE TIME

MATHEMATICS

TEACHER: If you had 36 cents in one pocket and 59 cents in the other pocket, what would you have?

BRAD: Somebody else's pants.

★   ★   ★

TEACHER: How do you find the square root of 144?

CARLA: I generally ask someone who's smarter than I am.

★   ★   ★

TEACHER: If you had two dimes and your brother gave you a nickel, how much money would you have?

HANS: Twenty cents.

TEACHER: You don't know your mathematics.

HANS: You don't know my brother.

★   ★   ★

TEACHER: Remember, class, you can't add apples and oranges.

RORY: My mother does it all the time. She calls it fruit cocktail.

TEACHER: If you have 5 people and only 4 apples, how would you divide them?

PETER: I'd ask someone to go get a knife and whoever was stupid enough to go wouldn't get an apple.

★   ★   ★

TEACHER: Let X equal the unknown quantity. Now, if $X + 10 = 20$, and $X - 5 = 5$, what is X?

EDWARD: As far as I'm concerned, it's still the unknown quantity.

★ ★ ★

TEACHER: Can you count from 1 to 20?

MARJORIE: I'm not sure. How about if I just count from 1 to 10 twice?

★ ★ ★

TEACHER: Today we're studying percentages. If there are ten questions on a quiz and you get ten correct, what do you get?

DALE: Accused of cheating.

★ ★ ★

SOCIAL STUDIES

TEACHER: On the test you said there were 51 states in the United States of America.

BRENDA: That's because when I was taking the test, I was in the state of confusion.

★ ★ ★

TEACHER: Go to the world globe and show me where you live.

RITA: I can't, Teacher. This globe doesn't have a basement.

★ ★ ★

TEACHER: Where do we find elephants?
CLARK: You can find them anywhere. They're very hard to hide.

★ ★ ★

TEACHER: What's the difference between an Indian elephant and an African elephant?
BARRY: Their zip codes.

★ ★ ★

TEACHER: Name three animals that give milk.
LOIS: The goat, the cow, and Mr. Miller who runs the dairy counter at the supermarket.

★ ★ ★

TEACHER: On which side of the globe is Central America?
JEFF: On the outside.

★ ★ ★

TEACHER: Can you tell me where the North and South Poles are?

SHEILA: Teacher, I'd have to go to the ends of the world to give you that answer.

★   ★   ★

TEACHER: Did you know that water covers two-thirds of our planet?

ALICE: Certainly—that's why the ocean is always less crowded than the beach.

★   ★   ★

My father grounded me for flunking Social Studies. How am I supposed to learn more about the world if I'm not allowed to leave my room?

★   ★   ★

SPELLING

TEACHER: Spell "weather."

SETH: Weather. W-A-E-F-H-A-R. Weather.

TEACHER: That's the worst spell of weather we've had in a long time.

★   ★   ★

TEACHER: Errol, for your homework, I asked you to spell "tomorrow" and you spelled "today."

ERROL: That's because I did my homework yesterday.

★   ★   ★

TEACHER: Can you spell "banana"?
DIANA: Banana. B-A-N-A-N-A-N-A-N. . . . I can spell it, all right—I just don't know where to stop.

★ ★ ★

TEACHER: Spell "javelin."
HERBERT: That's too hard and long for me.
TEACHER: And I guess you're not that sharp, either.

★ ★ ★

TEACHER: Can you spell "caterpillar?"
CAROL: How long do I have?
TEACHER: Why?
CAROL: I want to wait until he changes into a butterfly. I can spell that.

★ ★ ★

SCIENCE

TEACHER: Who is Isaac Newton?
CLAUDE: I have no idea, but I've heard of his brother, Fig.

★ ★ ★

TEACHER: Tell me which law of physics stops your car.
NINA: When my father is driving, it's usually a policeman who stops our car.

★ ★ ★

TEACHER: Tell me why the law of gravity is useful.
GLEN: If we drop something, it's much easier to get it off the floor than off the ceiling.

★　★　★

TEACHER: What type of animal is the bat?
DAVID: It's a mouse who went to pilot training school.

TEACHER: What does the term "extinct" mean?
CLAIRE: A dead skunk.

★　★　★

NED: What happened to the skunk who backed into the electric fan?
TED: He got cut off without a scent.

★　★　★

TEACHER: What is H_2O?
RALPH: Water.
TEACHER: What is H_2O_4?
RALPH: To drink.

★ ★ ★

TEACHER: What is a chemical formula?
GRETA: That's what married chemists feed to their new baby.

★ ★ ★

FATHER: Did you finish your chemistry experiment?
SON: Yes—with a bang.

★ ★ ★

TEACHER: What was that loud noise I just heard?
LEE: I think that was the chemistry class flunking their exam.

FATHER: How did you do in your chemistry experiment?

SON: I don't know. The teacher hasn't come down yet.

★   ★   ★

ENGLISH

TEACHER: Why should we never use the word "ain't?"

ROD: Because it ain't correct.

★   ★   ★

JOE: I know English good.

MOE: I know English *well.*

JOE: Good, then both of us ain't gonna flunk the exam.

★   ★   ★

TEACHER: Use the word "hyphenated" in a sentence.

EVA: There used to be just a space between these two words but there ain't no more because the hyphen ate it.

★   ★   ★

TEACHER: Mark, please stand and use the word "deceit" in a sentence.

MARK: I would rather sit down because "deceit" of my pants has a hole in it.

★   ★   ★

TEACHER: What do two negatives make?

PAUL: A double exposure.

★   ★   ★

8.
MAKING THE GRADES

In school, grades are necessary. In my case, they're a necessary evil.

★   ★   ★

The teacher gave me an F-minus. She says I not only didn't learn anything this year, but I probably forgot most of the stuff I learned last year.

★   ★   ★

In a class of 21 students, I finished 24th. Two of the desks got better grades than I got.

★   ★   ★

The lowest point in the United States used to be Death Valley—until my grades came out.

★   ★   ★

My grades are so low I have to get down on my knees to read my report card.

I'm doing so badly in school, I have to do extra credit work just to flunk.

★   ★   ★

I'll give you an idea how badly I'm doing in class. If I drop out of school, my grades go up.

★   ★   ★

My grades are so low, the only way I can graduate is to buy the school.

★   ★   ★

The only thing I've passed so far in the fifth grade is my tenth birthday.

★   ★   ★

My teacher says I might as well stay home from school. It's the first thing we've agreed on all year.

★ ★ ★

My teacher gave me an "f". She said I didn't deserve a capital letter.

★ ★ ★

I flunked every subject I took. I may not be smart, but I'm really consistent.

★ ★ ★

My fifth-grade teacher said that she and I have something in common—we'll both be back in the fifth grade next year.

★ ★ ★

I got straight "F's" in the sixth grade. That's not good, but it's a slight improvement over what I did in the sixth grade last year.

★ ★ ★

I was thrilled because I got my first "A" in school yesterday. Then I found out it meant "Absent."

★ ★ ★

My grades in school are so low I consider "A" a foreign language.

★ ★ ★

DONALD: Dad, that teacher flunked me because he doesn't like me. I can read him like an open book.

FATHER: Judging from these grades, I don't think you know what an open book looks like.

★ ★ ★

The only way I can ever get an "A" is to go on "Wheel of Fortune" and buy one.

★ ★ ★

This one teacher is so tough with grades, I brought my parents to school to talk to her about it. She flunked them.

TESS: Teacher, I was not feeling well the day I took this test.

TEACHER: I can believe that. Some of the answers you gave made me a little sick, too.

★ ★ ★

FRED: Teacher, I'm a good student and I deserve better than a "D".

TEACHER: What grade would you like?

FRED: Let's see—what's that letter that comes after "A" again?

★ ★ ★

ADAM: Teacher, you gave me a zero on this exam. Don't I even get anything for showing up?

TEACHER: What do you think brought you up to a zero?

★   ★   ★

My parents are so ashamed of my grades that on parent-teacher night, they came in disguise.

One teacher is a real tough grader. She once took 20 points off my grade because I didn't cross my "t's" and dot my "i's"—and it was an oral report.

★   ★   ★

My Dad thinks an "F" on a report card means "Throw a Fit."

★   ★   ★

When I showed my Dad my report card I said, "Remember, Dad, Thomas Edison got bad grades in school, too." He said, "Fine, stay in your room until you invent the light bulb."

★   ★   ★

My Dad hit the ceiling when I showed him my last report card. If I could only get my grades to go as high as he does!

★   ★   ★

FATHER: Judging from this report card, I think you'd better stay in your room every night doing homework.

NICHOLAS: Why? Judging from my report card, it's obviously not getting me anywhere.

★   ★   ★

SONJA: Dad, do you think I can still get into college?

FATHER: With these grades, you'll be lucky to get back into school Monday.

★   ★   ★

GREGORY: Teacher, how can I get into college with the grades you're giving me?

TEACHER: Probably as a janitor.

9.
THESE BOOKS ARE NOT FOR READING

TEACHER: Where is South America?
CHLOE: I don't know.
TEACHER: Where is Greenland?
CHLOE: I don't know.
TEACHER: Where is Bulgaria?
CHLOE: I don't know.
TEACHER: Look them up in your textbook.
CHLOE: I don't know where that is, either.

★　★　★

TEACHER: What does your history book tell you about the Civil War?
OLIVER: It doesn't tell me anything. I have to read the dumb thing.

★　★　★

TEACHER: What did you learn from your history book about Harriet Beecher Stowe?

KAREN: If you draw a beard and a stovepipe hat on her, she looks exactly like Abraham Lincoln.

★   ★   ★

TEACHER: Alex, why are you holding your textbook up to the window?

ALEX: You told me to open it up to the Middle East.

★   ★   ★

If you don't know what the word "dictionary" means, where would you look it up?

★   ★   ★

My Father gave me a really cheap dictionary for my birthday. I couldn't find the words to thank him.

★   ★   ★

JASPER: How many books have you read in your lifetime?

CASPER: I don't know. I'm not dead yet.

★   ★   ★

TEACHER: Gracie, how many books did you finish over the summer?

GRACIE: None. My brother stole my box of crayons.

★   ★   ★

LIBRARIAN: Why don't you take home a Dr. Seuss?

MAURICE: I didn't know he made house calls.

★   ★   ★

TEACHER: Who is your favorite author?
TERRY: George Washington.
TEACHER: But George Washington never wrote any books.
TERRY: You got it.

★ ★ ★

TEACHER: Connie, tell the class what book you read and then tell them something about the plot.
CONNIE: I read "The Life of Thomas Jefferson." He dies at the end.

★ ★ ★

TEACHER: Frannie, tell the class what book you read and what you thought of it.
FRANNIE: I read the phone book, but I didn't understand it. It had too many characters.

★ ★ ★

Our school library is so quiet you can hear a pin drop—and if it does, the pin will be sent to the principal's office.

★ ★ ★

LIBRARIAN: Did you enjoy reading *The Hunchback of Notre Dame*?
MORRIS: Well, I read the first 100 pages, then I found out it wasn't about football.

★ ★ ★

TEACHER: Tell the class what book you read.
HARRIET: *Black Beauty.*
TEACHER: And tell the class what it was about.
HARRIET: It was about 120 pages.

★ ★ ★

DICK: Do you have *Oliver Twist* in hard cover?

LIBRARIAN: Yes, we do.

DICK: Well, let him out; he's a friend of mine.

★   ★   ★

LIBRARIAN: Did you enjoy reading *Moby Dick*?

ANITA: I couldn't finish it. I got seasick.

★   ★   ★

SEYMOUR: Do you have *Moby Dick*?

LIBRARIAN: Yes, we do.

SEYMOUR: I thought something smelled fishy in here.

Our school library is so quiet, when I'm sitting in there, I can hear my hair grow.

★   ★   ★

Our school librarian is very strict. She'll send you to the principal's office for thinking too loudly.

★   ★   ★

My teacher says our schoolbooks are a magic carpet that will take us all over the world. I took mine to the garage and had them fitted with seat belts.

All of my schoolbooks have pictures in them—even if I have to draw them myself.

★   ★   ★

My teacher caught me drawing in my American Revolution textbook. She said, "What do you think you're doing?" I said, "Making my mark in history."

★   ★   ★

One of my teachers said that I should hand in my books at the end of the year better than when I got them. What does he want me to do—add pages?

★   ★   ★

My teacher told us that books are man's best friend, so my dog bit him.

★   ★   ★

My teacher says we should treat our schoolbooks just like we treat one another. So after school, I picked a fight with my History book.

★   ★   ★

MOTHER: How come you never bring any books home?

WENDELL: Mom, they're schoolbooks, not home books.

★   ★   ★

KENNETH: Dad, my teacher says I should have an encyclopedia.

FATHER: Nonsense, you'll walk to school the same as I did.

★   ★   ★

The only thing I hate worse than carrying a lot of schoolbooks home is having to open them once I get there.

★   ★   ★

If the Good Lord wanted us to bring schoolbooks home from school, He would have put wheels on them.

★   ★   ★

Any book with George Washington's writing in it is worth thousands of dollars. Any book with my writing in it is worth two weeks of detention.

★   ★   ★

My lunch leaked all over my schoolbooks. I now have the only geography book where the map of Turkey is covered with gravy.

★   ★   ★

We have to carry heavy books home—then we have to carry heavy books back to school in the morning. If the authorities knew this was going to happen, why didn't they build the school closer to us?

★   ★   ★

10.
TIME OUT

Our teacher said we could do anything we wanted during recess—so I moved to Pittsburgh.

     ★   ★   ★

Just my luck. Recess is the only thing in school I'm good at and they don't give grades in it.

     ★   ★   ★

I like recess so much, when I go to college, I may major in it.

     ★   ★   ★

Recess is what I've decided to do with the rest of my life.

     ★   ★   ★

The teacher came to me one day during recess and said, "You're doing nothing but wasting your time." I said, "I'm sorry. Whose time should I be wasting?"

★　★　★

TEACHER: How can I get you to devote as much energy to your class work as you devote to recess?

GARY: Start playing dodge ball in class.

MOTHER: You can't play those rough games in the 5th grade. You'll get yourself killed.

STEVE: Oh no, Mom. That's the game they play in the 6th grade.

★　★　★

TEACHER: What's your favorite class in school?
PEGGY: Morning recess.
TEACHER: What's your favorite class after that?
PEGGY: Tomorrow morning's recess.

★   ★   ★

We play games at recess in our school. One class-mate suggested a game of "Hide and Seek." We didn't find him for four months.

★   ★   ★

MOTHER: You have a bloody nose. Were you fighting in school again today?
BRUCE: No, I wasn't fighting, but the kid who hit me in the nose sure was.

★   ★   ★

TEACHER: Who started the fight?
GLENDA: He did, Teacher. He purposely hit me back.

★   ★   ★

WES: What's the highest you ever did at jumping rope?
JESS: Oh, about two inches off the ground.

★   ★   ★

JESS: Do you jump rope much?
WES: No, just once each time the rope comes around.

★   ★   ★

I'm very good at jumping rope. Oh, I miss a lot, but it's generally the rope's fault.

★   ★   ★

I hold the school record for jumping rope—One. No one's ever done lower than that.

★   ★   ★

BEN: Every time I throw a Frisbee, the dog jumps up and catches it.

KEN: That sounds like fun.

BEN: It's getting pretty expensive, you know. It's not my dog.

★　★　★

When we choose up sides for ball games, nobody ever chooses me. Both teams would rather chip in and send me to a movie.

★　★　★

Nobody likes to have me on their team. We chose up sides yesterday and Joey Masters was chosen before me—and he moved to Omaha three years ago.

★　★　★

LOUIS: Hey captain, where do you want me to play?

CAPTAIN: How about at another school?

★　★　★

ANDY: I can't play ball today. I caught a cold.

CAPTAIN: Congratulations. That's the first thing you've caught all year.

★　★　★

I'm not good at anything that requires coordination. Even my dog can play dead better than I can.

★　★　★

11.
KOOKY CLASSMATES

I know one kid who will do absolutely anything to get the teachers to like him—even homework.

★　★　★

One kid in our class was so stupid he had his address tattooed on his forehead. That way, when he got lost he could mail himself home.

★　★　★

Another kid was so stupid he had "left" and "right" tattooed on his toes so he would know which feet his shoes should go on. Now all he has to do is learn how to read.

★　★　★

I knew a person who was so stupid, the only way he got out of the third grade was to marry the teacher.

★　★　★

One kid in our class was really stupid. He was late for school every day because he kept trying to put his pants on over his head.

I had one friend who was a real dummy. He lost his shoes one time because he put them on the wrong feet. Then he couldn't remember whose feet he put them on.

★　★　★

One classmate of mine is so stupid he puts his eyeglasses on backwards. He wants to see where he's been, not where he's going.

★　★　★

One kid in our class is so dense, he took his dog to obedience school. The dog passed; he flunked.

★　★　★

One classmate doesn't carry a pocket comb. He says none of his pockets need combing.

★　★　★

We have one really stupid classmate. The football coach told him to jog three miles every day. The last time we heard from him he was somewhere around Wichita, Kansas.

★　★　★

One classmate is so stupid he can't even dress himself yet. He can only dress other people.

★　★　★

One of our classmates is so stupid he always carries a spare tire—just in case he ever buys a car without one.

★　★　★

One kid in our class is so dense he can't fill in his name on an application form unless it's a multiple-choice question.

★　★　★

One of my classmates is dangerously stupid. He wanted to have his address tattooed on the inside of his eyelids so he could find his way home with his eyes closed.

★　★　★

We have one classmate who is really a dimwit. His mother once bought him some Silly Putty to play with and it outsmarted him.

★　★　★

One guy in our class is smarter than Einstein. Of course, so am I, but he's smarter than Einstein when he was alive.

★   ★   ★

I'm very smart in school. I have a photographic memory. That means any time I want to know anything, I drop my brain off at Fotomat and it takes a week to ten days to get it back.

. . . It usually comes back blurry.

★   ★   ★

A classmate of mine is so smart, he knows the answer to every question the teacher asks. He raises his hand so often in class that his under-arms are sunburned.

★   ★   ★

We have a kid in our class who's so smart, he's got more brains in his little finger than I have in my entire family.

★   ★   ★

We have a really mean kid in our school. He goes to "Rambo" movies and roots for the ammunition.

★   ★   ★

One kid in our class gets in a fight every day after school. He says it helps keep him out of trouble.

★   ★   ★

Bullies are nothing more than cowards—who can beat the stuffings out of the rest of us.

12.
BREAKING THE DRESS CODE

We have a very simple dress code at our school. Anything that's comfortable or looks cool is illegal.

★   ★   ★

Our school has a strict dress code. The only time we can dress the way we like is on Halloween.

★   ★   ★

The dress code at our school is simple—if you're not taken for one of the teachers, you're in trouble.

★   ★   ★

Our school has a very strict dress code. Laced shoes, pressed trousers, shirt and tie—and that's just the girls.

★   ★   ★

Our school has a simple rule as a dress code. If your parents wouldn't wear it, then you can't.

★   ★   ★

My parents are very relaxed. I can wear anything I want—provided I don't leave the house.

★   ★   ★

Our school adopted such a strict dress code that the first week, three of the teachers were kept after school.

We have a very strict dress code at our school. Yesterday my lunch was punished because they said the brown paper bag it came in was offensive.

★　★　★

One kid in our class is a real sloppy dresser. He tried to give some of his old clothes to Good Will. They gave them back.

★　★　★

One classmate is a real sloppy dresser. You've heard the expression, "Cleanliness is next to Godliness"? Well, with this kid it's next to impossible.

★　★　★

One guy is such a sloppy dresser—if you ever see him when his shirttail is *not* hanging out, it means he's not wearing a shirt.

★　★　★

One kid in our class dresses terribly. The only things that match on him are his belt size and his I.Q.

★　★　★

One kid wears clothes that have so many rips, he can clip his toenails with his shoes and socks still on.

★　★　★

One classmate dresses so sloppily, when he was in a minor accident, they sent him home and took his clothes to the emergency ward.

★　★　★

It's hard to describe the clothing this one class-mate of mine wears, but if you saw it growing in your garden, you'd spray it with weed killer.

. . . if you saw it running across your kitchen floor, your father would hit it with a broom.

. . . if you found it in your refrigerator, you'd toss it in the garbage disposal.

★   ★   ★

One kid wears clothes that are so wrecked, the tailor won't even repair them. He has to take them to a body and fender shop.

★   ★   ★

One guy wears a tie to school every day. Now if they could only get him to wear a shirt.

Another kid I know just wears clothes badly. He could go to a nudist camp and be dressed wrong.

★   ★   ★

We have a kid in class who dresses like a million bucks. Everything he wears is all wrinkled and green.

★   ★   ★

The teacher told one of the bad dressers in our class to do something about his shirttail hanging out. So he took off his pants.

★   ★   ★

TEACHER: Lester, I think you have your shoes on the wrong feet.

LESTER: No I don't, teacher. These are the only feet I have.

★   ★   ★

This one kid in our class is really proud of the way he looks. He invited himself to the Spring Dance.

★   ★   ★

One kid in our class wears the best of everything. Even in gym class he has designer sweat.

★   ★   ★

One girl in our class is a very neat dresser. She stayed home sick one day because her skirt was mussed.

★   ★   ★

One girl is very neat. She gives her clothes away to the needy when they get wrinkled.

★   ★   ★

One girl in our class is a nut about neatness. Her blouse got a food stain on it one day at lunch. She took it out and shot it.

★   ★   ★

13.
THE SCHOOL
CAFETERIA

We had mashed potatoes and gravy in the school cafeteria today, and no one could tell them apart.

*   *   *

The food in our school cafeteria is so bad, they sell gravy by the slice.

*   *   *

The only good thing about the gravy in our school lunchroom is that it hides the rest of the food.

*   *   *

I asked for gravy in the school cafeteria today and they said, "One lump or two?"

* * *

The gravy they serve at school is so thick, when they try to stir it, the cafeteria spins around.

* * *

The gravy in our school lunchroom is so thick, you have to get a friend to help you soak your bread in it.

* * *

The roast beef we had in the cafeteria today was harder than the test we had in history yesterday.

* * *

The meat was so tough at lunch today, half the class was kept after school so we could finish chewing it.

* * *

I've had tough slices of meat before, but this one stood up and challenged me to a fight after school.

* * *

The roast beef they serve in the school cafeteria is so thin and tough, none of the kids eat it. We use it for knee patches.

* * *

The food in our school lunchroom is so bad that teachers hand out second helpings as punishment.

* * *

I saw the recipe for the stew they serve in our school lunchroom. It begins: "Take the ingredients from last week . . ."

★   ★   ★

NED: Did you see the stew they served in the cafeteria today?

TED: No, but I'll see it when they serve it again next week.

★   ★   ★

Let me try to describe what the food tastes like in our school cafeteria. Have you ever eaten any of your old clothes?

★   ★   ★

They served chicken noodle soup in the school cafeteria today. A kid from the third grade got the noodle.

★   ★   ★

ALBERT: Do they have good food in your school cafeteria?

TALBOT: Yeah, until somebody cooks it.

★   ★   ★

TEACHER: What was the Tuesday Special in the cafeteria?

RAMONA: Meat loaf.

TEACHER: How did it taste?

RAMONA: Like it should have been the Monday Special.

★   ★   ★

The food in our school lunchroom is so bad, most of the kids say grace before, during, and after the meal.

★   ★   ★

If we ever study ancient history, the cafeteria will have the rolls to go with it.

*   *   *

Every Friday in our school cafeteria, they serve leftovers—from World War II.

*   *   *

The food is so bad in the school cafeteria that flies go there to lose weight.

*   *   *

NELLIE: How do they keep flies out of the kitchen in the school cafeteria?

KELLY: They let them taste the food.

I'll give you an idea how bad the food is in our school—when's the last time you saw hot dogs served with their tails between their legs?

*   *   *

They threw out the leftovers from the school cafeteria yesterday. All the alley cats in the neighborhood threw it back.

The cook at our school wrote a cookbook. They say it's the kind of book that once you read it, you can't keep it down.

★　　★　　★

Another cook at our school cafeteria tried to write a cookbook, but it came out of the typewriter burnt.

★　　★　　★

MOLLY: What's the best thing they've ever had in your school cafeteria?
POLLY: A fire drill.

★　　★　　★

DICK: What is this we're eating?

RICK: It looks like small chunks of chicken and large chunks of gravy.

★ ★ ★

JAY: What's the best thing to have in the school cafeteria?

MAY: An excused absence.

★ ★ ★

TEACHER: What do you get when you mix hydrogen chloride and potassium sulfate?

JUSTIN: The gravy they served in the cafeteria today.

★ ★ ★

CASSIE: Excuse me, M'am, but I'd like to know what's in today's stew.

SCHOOL COOK: No, you wouldn't.

★ ★ ★

RAMON: Today's meal looks like spaghetti and meatballs.

WAYNE: Oh, good. For a minute there I thought it was shoelaces and hockey pucks.

★ ★ ★

We had a food fight in the school cafeteria today. The food won.

★ ★ ★

Our school cafeteria discourages food fights. The food they serve there is dangerous enough without throwing it.

Someone might accidentally swallow the food.

★ ★ ★

The food in our school cafeteria is so bad, last night they caught a mouse trying to phone out for a pizza.

BOB: They served Tuna Surprise sandwiches in the school lunchroom today.

ROB: I thought they were just Tuna sandwiches.

BOB: They were. The surprise comes about an hour after you eat them.

★   ★   ★

Kids in our school love to start food fights. Anything is better than eating the cafeteria food.

★   ★   ★

TEACHER: You children should be ashamed of having a food fight in the cafeteria. Do you have any idea what goes into preparing your food?

SHARON: No, teacher. That's why we started throwing it instead of eating it.

★ ★ ★

TEACHER: When I asked who was involved in the food fight, why didn't you raise your hand?

MILTON: I couldn't hear you, teacher. I had mashed potatoes in my ear.

★ ★ ★

TEACHER: What started that food fight in the cafeteria?

TRACY: It started with the salad, then the meat loaf, and it ended with the dessert.

★ ★ ★

TEACHER: I can't understand why anyone would want to throw their food around the cafeteria.

BERT: Have you tasted the food?

14.
LATE AGAIN!

TEACHER: Young woman, do you know what time we start school here in the morning?

JOANNE: No, teacher, I don't. I've never been here for that.

     ★   ★   ★

TEACHER: Young man, you've been late for school every day this week.

ALVIN: No, teacher, I was only late for school four days this week. The other day I was absent.

     ★   ★   ★

TEACHER: Do you have any idea how many times you've been late for school this year?

CLIFF: Well, teacher, I don't think it's been more than once a day.

★ ★ ★

TEACHER: Young man, you've been late for school five days this week. Does that make you happy?

MARIO: Sure does—that means it's Friday.

★ ★ ★

TEACHER: Young lady, do you know what the word "tardy" means?

VILMA: No, teacher, I don't. You must have covered that before I got here.

★ ★ ★

TEACHER: Young man, how would you like it if I were ten minutes late for school every morning like you are?

TODD: It would be great. We could ride to school together.

★ ★ ★

TEACHER: You've been ten minutes late for school every day this year and all you do is come up with stupid excuses.

MARY LOU: I know. If I could be 15 minutes late, that would give me enough time to come up with better excuses.

★ ★ ★

One kid in our class is always late for school. When we studied the Hundred Years War, he only showed up for the last three years.

★ ★ ★

TEACHER: Do you have a good excuse for being absent yesterday?

PHIL: If I had a *good* excuse for being absent, I'd save it and use it for tomorrow.

★ ★ ★

TEACHER: You were absent yesterday and I want a note from your doctor.

HAL: All right, I'll take off from school tomorrow and get one for you.

★ ★ ★

NANCY: Did you hear the good news? The Principal gave us the day off from school tomorrow.

HOWARD: Doggone it, and I was planning to skip school tomorrow.

★ ★ ★

TEACHER: Because of your absences you've missed three tests this week.

RUTHIE: No, I may not have taken the tests, but I didn't miss them one bit.

★ ★ ★

TEACHER: Why are you so grouchy today?

JERRY: I got up on the wrong side of the bed this morning.

TEACHER: And that makes you grouchy?

JERRY: Sure it does. My bed is next to the wall.

★ ★ ★

BORIS: What does it take for your Mom to get you out of bed in the morning?

NORRIS: About 45 minutes.

★ ★ ★

82

My father has a great way of getting me out of bed in the morning. I sleep with the two dogs in my bed and when it's time for me to get up, he throws the cat in.

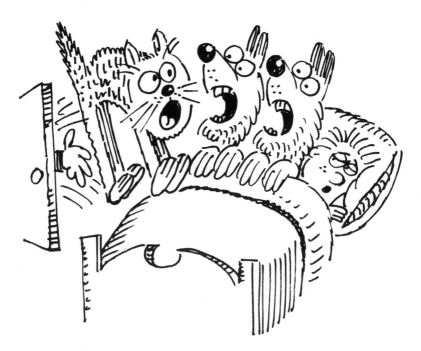

I like to sleep. That not only explains why I'm late to school, but also my grades.

★   ★   ★

I'm always prompt at getting out of bed in the morning. I figure the sooner I get to school, the sooner I can get back to sleep.

★   ★   ★

This kid in our class is never on time for anything. He was four hours late catching the 24-hour virus.

★   ★   ★

We have a kid in our school who has never been on time for anything. He was two years old when he was born.

★ ★ ★

I have another buddy who is late for everything. It takes her an hour and a half to watch *60 Minutes.*

★ ★ ★

AMY: My father's a doctor, so I can stay home and be sick for nothing.

DENNIS: My father's a preacher, so I can stay home and be good for nothing.

★ ★ ★

I had a dream last night that I was eating this giant marshmallow. When I woke up, my pillow was gone.

WINNIE: You know, you were in one of the dreams I had last night.

MINNIE: Oh, that explains it. I was missing from one of mine.

★　★　★

DEAN: Every morning I dream I'm falling from a 10-story building and just before I hit the ground, I wake up.

GENE: That's terrible. What are you going to do about it?

DEAN: I'm going to move into a 15-story building. I need more sleep.

★　★　★

15.
GETTING INTO TROUBLE

TEACHER: Naomi, I don't know what I'm going to do with you.

NAOMI: Now you know how I felt yesterday during the math exam.

★　★　★

TEACHER: You're in real trouble now, Young Man.

FRANKLIN: Good. I hate to bring my parents to the Principal's office for *fake* trouble.

★　★　★

TEACHER: Mr. and Mrs. Smith, I'm sorry that I have to bring you here to school so often.

MRS. SMITH: Oh, that's quite all right. This is the only time we get to go out.

* * *

TEACHER: Mrs. Jones, your son is a constant trouble maker. How do you put up with him?

MRS. JONES: I can't. That's why I send him to school.

* * *

TEACHER: Mrs. Johnson, your son is a trouble maker and we'd like to know what you're going to do about it.

MRS. JOHNSON: I don't have time to do anything about it. I'm too busy running back and forth to school.

* * *

FATHER TO SON: I wish you'd learn to behave yourself. I spend more time in school as your father than I did when I was a student.

* * *

ANDREA: I don't know what it is, Dad. Every time I turn around they want me to bring my parents to school.

FATHER: Stop turning around.

* * *

I had a friend who was kept after school so much, his parents rented out his room.

* * *

I have a classmate who's in so much trouble at school, he made the PTA's "Ten Most Wanted" list.

I know a kid who's always in trouble at school. He may not graduate; he may just be paroled.

★   ★   ★

TEACHER: Sometimes I think you come to school just to cause trouble.

LEROY: No, but I figure as long as I'm here . . .

★   ★   ★

TEACHER: Young man, I'm going to give you a punishment you won't soon forget.

JONATHAN: Good, because I sure can't remember anything you teach us.

★   ★   ★

TEACHER: Matthew, you're the number one trouble maker in this class.

MATTHEW: See? And my parents said I'd never amount to anything.

★   ★   ★

TEACHER: Phoebe, every time I turn around I catch you doing something you're not supposed to be doing. What can we do about that?

PHOEBE: Tell me when you're going to turn around.

★ ★ ★

TEACHER: You were told to bring your parents to school today. Where are they?

ANGELA: They wouldn't come. They don't like school any more than I do.

★ ★ ★

TEACHER: I want you to bring your parents to school tomorrow.

DUSTIN: I don't think they can make it. Would my parole officer do?

★ ★ ★

I know one kid who has to bring her parents to school so often, they have a better attendance record than she has.

★ ★ ★

I knew one kid who was always being kept after school. When they finally let him go home, he forgot where he lived.

★ ★ ★

One buddy of mine was always being kept after school. He spent so much time at school, they delivered his mail there.

★ ★ ★

TEACHER: Jason, I want you to report to the Principal's office.

JASON: But I didn't do anything.

TEACHER: I know, but this will save you a trip when you do.

★   ★   ★

One kid in class drew a picture of our teacher on the blackboard. It got her in serious trouble because it looked just like him.

★   ★   ★

I had one classmate who was always in trouble. He got one day when he didn't have to stay after school. He went to his house and said, "Mom and Dad, I'm home." They said, "That's nice, but who are you?"

★   ★   ★

One buddy of mine was kept after school so often, when his family moved to a new town, it took him three months to find out.

★   ★   ★

One buddy of mine was always being kept after school. The only thing he ever learned in school was how to lock up when he left.

★   ★   ★

One of my buddies has been kept after school so much, the only time he sees the outside world is during fire drills.

★   ★   ★

16.
THE LAST DAY OF SCHOOL

FRITZ: I plan to do absolutely nothing for the next three months.

TEACHER: That should be easy. You've had nine months of practice doing that in school.

★   ★   ★

Summer vacation is tough. We only have three months to forget what it took us nine months of school to learn.

★   ★   ★

KIM: Teacher, it's the last day of school. This is the day I've been dreaming about for a long time.

TEACHER: I know. You did a lot of that dreaming in class.

★ ★ ★

I'm glad they don't get Groundhog Day and the last day of school mixed up. I'd hate to see my shadow and have six more weeks of classes.

LUKE: During my vacation I'm going to do all the things I couldn't do during the school year.

DUKE: Like what—pass English?

★ ★ ★

TONY: I'm going to spend my vacation reviewing everything I learned at school.

JOANIE: Really? What are you going to do the second day?

★ ★ ★

LAURIE: My teacher says that summer vacation is not the time to stop learning.

MAURIE: I agree. I stopped learning way before the Christmas break.

SOME LAST DAY OF SCHOOL CHANTS

No more pencils.
No more books.
No more teachers'
Dirty looks.

        ★   ★   ★

School is over.
School is done.
We can stop learning
And start having fun.

        ★   ★   ★

Readin', 'Ritin', and 'Rithmatic.
Nine months of that can make you sick.

        ★   ★   ★

Readin', Writin',
  And History—
Nine months of that's
  Enough for me.

★   ★   ★

What did I learn?
I don't remember.
And I'm not gonna try
Till next September.

★   ★   ★

No more pens
No more ink.
No more tests
And having to think.

★   ★   ★

Roses are red;
Violets are blue.
School is over.
Toodle-oo.

INDEX